Crafts

Candle Making

Work with Wicks and Wax

by Deborah Hufford

Capstone press

Snap Books are published by Capstone Press,
151 Good Counsel Drive, P.O. Box 669, Mankato, Minnesota 56002
www.capstonepress.com

Library of Congress Cataloging-in-Publication Data
Hufford, Deborah.
  Candle making: work with wicks and wax / by Deborah Hufford.— 1st ed.
    p. cm. — (Snap books crafts)
  Includes index.
  ISBN 0-7368-4383-3 (hardcover)
  1. Candlemaking. I. Title. II. Series.
  TT896.5H84 2005
  745.593'32 — dc22   2005006908

Summary: A do-it-yourself crafts book for children and pre-teens on candle making.

Editors: Thea Feldman; Deb Berry/Bill SMITH STUDIO
Illustrators: Lisa Parett; Roxanne Daner, Marina Terletsky and Brock Waldron/Bill SMITH STUDIO
Designers: Roxanne Daner, Marina Terletsky, and Brock Waldron/Bill SMITH STUDIO
Photo Researcher: Iris Wong/Bill SMITH STUDIO

Photo Credits: Cover: (girl) PhotoDisc & Tim Hicken; 4 PhotoDisc; 6 PhotoDisc; 8 (b) PhotoDisc, (tc) Artville;
9 PhotoDisc; 10 Mel Yates/Getty Images; 15 Corel; 17 (bl) PhotoDisc; (br) Richard Hutchings Photography;
19 PhotoDisc; 24 (bc) PhotoDisc; 25 (c) PhotoDisc ; 26 (br) Artville; 28 (bl & tr) Clipart.com;
32 (tr) Courtesy Deborah Hufford; All other photos Tim Hicken.

1 2 3 4 5 6 10 09 08 07 06 05

Table of Contents

Go Metric!

It's easy to change measurements
to metric! Just use this chart.

To change	into	multiply by
inches	centimeters	2.54
inches	millimeters	25.4
feet	meters	.305
yards	meters	.914
ounces (liquid)	milliliters	29.57
ounces (liquid)	liters	.029
cups (liquid)	liters	.237
pints	liters	.473
quarts	liters	.946
gallons	liters	3.78
ounces (dry)	grams	28.35
pounds	grams	453.59

CHAPTER 1

Let There Be Light

Candles are a bright idea.

Candles add warmth to everyday life and to special occasions. Today, candle making is a fun and popular hobby. You can make candles for gifts or use them to brighten your own life.

Safety First

The most important thing about making candles is observing basic safety rules.

* Follow directions on packaging for wax and other materials.

* Always have adult supervision when using the stove and working with hot, melted wax.

* Always use hot pads when handling hot, melted wax.

* Never leave anything unattended on stove.

* Always work on a steady surface, covered with tin foil or newspaper.

* Always have an adult light candles.

* Make sure candles are on steady surfaces, away from walls, curtains, and anything that might catch on fire.

* Always place molds with hot, melted wax in a sided pan to catch leaks.

CHAPTER 2

Wax, Wicks, and Whimsy

Shedding light on candle making

While every candle has wax and a wick, there are as many different kinds of candles as there are ways to make them. You can use removable **molds**, or put wax in containers that become part of the finished candle. The crafts in this book use **chunk wax**, **wax sheets**, **beeswax**, wax from **drip candles**, and **gel wax**.

Scent-sational

Make your candles smell wonderful by adding candle making scents to the wax just before pouring it into the mold. Be sure not to use perfumes with alcohol in them.

Pick of the Wicks

There are many kinds of wicks. The crafts in this book all use medium-sized, **pre-tabbed wicks**.

CHAPTER 3

Light Up Your Life!

With candles you make yourself!

You'll find other craft-specific materials listed with each project in this book.

Washed, empty tin cans are great for melting wax. Put wax in a coffee can (when melting a lot) or in a soup can (when melting a little).

Here's what you need to get started

* wax thermometer
* frying pan
* tin can(s)
* pencil
* scissors
* hot pads

Safety First

Be sure to check the temperature of melting wax with a wax thermometer. For most projects in this book, wax is ready to pour at 160° Fahrenheit (71.1° Celsius). If wax gets too hot, it can catch fire, so watch it carefully. If your wax does catch fire, don't pour water on it. Smother it with baking soda or a pan lid.

If you get hot wax on your skin, apply ice to the area immediately.

CHAPTER 4

Show Your Stripes

Bold bands of color are hot!

Here's a fun, fresh candle that can match your favorite room. And it's super easy to make. Just layer different colors of melted wax to create a look you love. This candle will brighten up your life even when it's not lit.

Think out of the Box for Molds

You can buy metal molds at craft stores, but you can also make molds out of some everyday household objects. The molds for these layered candles are: a toothpaste box, a baking powder can, a small orange juice can, and a small gift box.

REMEMBER!

Safety First

Always place molds with hot, melted wax in a sided pan to catch leaks.

Here's what you need

* wick
* pencil
* mold
* packaging or duct tape
* frying pan
* 5 soup cans
* 5 pounds white chunk wax
* different colors solid or liquid dye
* wax thermometer
* scissors
* hot pads

Here's what you do

1 Set wick (see page 13).

2 Fill frying pan half full of water.

3 Fill each tin can half full of chunk wax and place cans in frying pan.

4 Heat wax over low heat.

5 As wax melts, gradually add different colored drops of liquid dye or slivers of solid dye in each can to achieve desired colors.

6 Melt wax to 160° Fahrenheit (71.1° Celsius), monitoring temperature with wax thermometer.

7 Using hot pads, pour small amount of melted wax from one can into mold.

8 Place mold in freezer for 20 minutes or until wax hardens.

9 Repeat Steps 7 and 8 with other melted wax colors, as desired, to create additional layers.

10 When candle has hardened, tear off mold.

11 Trim wick to ½ inch.

Setting the Wick

Before pouring melted wax, "set" the wick by placing it with the metal tab down in the center of the mold. Anchor the wick by taping its top to a pencil placed across the mold's opening.

Where to Find Wax Thermometers

You can buy a wax thermometer (like the one pictured on page 12) at most craft stores. Candle supply stores on the Internet also carry them. But if you're still having trouble finding one, a candy thermometer, which looks very similar to a wax thermometer, will do just as well. You can buy candy thermometers in most stores that sell kitchen and cooking supplies.

CHAPTER 5

Season's Greetings!

Candles put cheer into your favorite season. Hooray!

Candles are everywhere during the holidays. Make **embedded candles** filled with things that remind you of your favorite time of year.

14

Here's what you need

* empty, washed, round oatmeal container

* 3-inch **column core candle**

* materials for embedding (see p. 17)

* 5 pounds white chunk wax

* coffee can

* frying pan

* wax thermometer

* hot pads

To make a square candle instead of a round one, place a 2½ inch square core candle inside of an empty, washed pint-sized cream carton. No matter what shape you choose, make sure there's at least ½ inch of space between the core candle and the mold.

Here's what you do

1 Center core candle inside mold.

2 Cut mold to same height as candle.

3 Spread embed materials evenly between core candle and mold.

4 Fill frying pan half full of water.

5 Fill coffee can three-quarters full of chunk wax, and place in frying pan.

6 Heat wax over low heat.

7 Melt wax to 160° Fahrenheit (71.1° Celsius), check temperature with wax thermometer.

8 Using hot pads, slowly pour melted wax into mold, distributing evenly around core candle until wax reaches candle height.

9 Place mold and candle in freezer about 30 minutes or until wax hardens.

10 When candle has hardened, tear off mold.

How to "Season" a Candle

Spring Use pastel jelly beans.

Summer Use bright silk flowers and leaves.

Fall Use brown coffee beans, white pinto beans, and yellow wax beans.

Winter Use plastic holly with berries or dried cranberries.

CHAPTER 6

Seeing Spots

This candle is so special, you can "spot" it anywhere.

Everyone will love this candle. The beautiful colors will brighten up any space, and you'll have a blast making the spots.

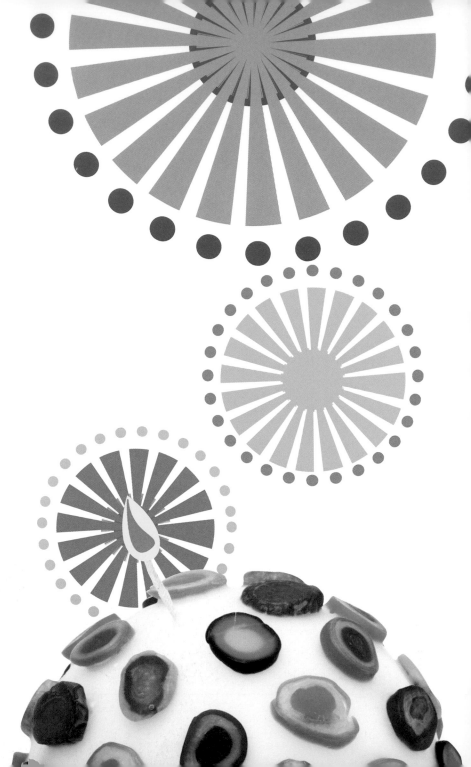

Here's what you need

* 3 to 6 differently colored wax sheets
* sharp knife
* wax glue
* 3-inch **ball candle**
* coffee can
* 5 pounds white chunk wax
* frying pan
* wax thermometer
* pliers
* hot pads

Here's what you do first

Make Spots!

1 Cut each wax sheet into 2-inch by 4-inch strips.

2 Role one wax strip lengthwise into a tight log or **cane**.

3 Wrap a wax strip in a second color around cane.

4 Repeat with third color.

5 Make more canes. Repeat Steps 1–4 with different color combinations.

6 Cut ⅛ inch slices (about the thickness of two small coins) off ends of canes.

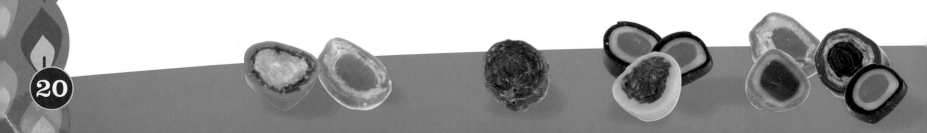

Here's what you do next

1 Glue dots to candle with wax glue.

2 Fill frying pan half full of water.

3 Fill coffee can three-quarters full of chunk wax, and place in frying pan.

4 Heat wax over low heat.

5 Melt wax to 160° Fahrenheit (71° Celsius), checking temperature with wax thermometer.

6 Use pliers to hold candle by wick, and quickly dunk candle, coating to hold dots in place.

7 Let candle dry about 30 minutes.

Checkerboard Chic

Give a plain candle a fabulous look with this tic-tac-toe pattern! Cut 1-inch squares out of beeswax sheets and glue them onto a column candle.

CHAPTER 7

Drizzle and Sizzle

Drip candles are mounds of fun!

Usually, when you think of something that drips, it's not a good thing. For example, no one likes a drippy faucet. But with drip candles, the drippier, the better! Create candles to match any mood by using color combos that sizzle with style.

Here's what you need

* any size pop bottle
* used, 4-inch-long **taper candle**
* 5 different colored **drip candles**

   If you can't find any brightly colored drip candles at your local craft store, you can buy them from stores on the Internet.

Here's what you do

1 Place used taper candle inside bottle opening.

2 Light a drip candle.

3 Hold drip candle sideways over top of bottle and cover bottle completely with wax.

4 Repeat Steps 4 and 5 with the rest of the candles, dripping wax evenly down sides of the bottle.

Wickedly Good Wick

Make a Halloween candle! Cover the top of a bottle with yellow wax, the middle with orange, and the base with black.

CHAPTER 8

Gone Fishin'

It's no fluke. This is a de-"lightful" container candle!

This amazing fish bowl candle will brighten any room. It's hard to contain your excitement about the look of this container candle.

Here's what you need

* 30-ounce glass fishbowl or glass container
* 1 pound blue glass, marbles, or sand
* wick
* scissors
* 2 cups small sea shells
* three to four little glass fish
* thread
* tape
* 40 ounces gel wax
* coffee can
* frying pan
* wax thermometer
* hot pads

Here's what you do

1. Pour ½ inch of blue glass, marbles, or sand in bottom of fishbowl.

2. Anchor wick in middle of fishbowl by placing shells around its metal disk.

3. Trim wick to ½ inch.

4. Loop thread through holes of little glass fish, and hang them inside bowl, taping thread on outside to hold fish in place.

5. Fill frying pan half full of water.

6. Fill coffee can with gel wax, and place in frying pan.

7. Heat wax over low heat.

8 Melt wax to 190° Fahrenheit (187.7° Celsius), monitoring temperature with wax thermometer.

9 Using hot pads, gently pour melted gel wax into glass container.

10 Allow wax to cool about 60 minutes.

11 Gently pull out threads.

Hot Wired

Unwind some decorative wire and crumple into a loose ball. Place inside a glass water goblet or other clear container. Run a wick down the middle of the wire and trim. Follow steps 5-10 from pages 26-27.

Fast Facts

From Whence Wax Came

The first candles were probably made from plants dipped in animal fat. In the 1700s, wax was made from whale blubber. Around 1850, wax was developed from crude oil, the way most candles are made today.

Candlefish

Early Native Americans threaded wicks through the mouth and down the length of oily fishes and used the fish as torches.

Bright Idea

Until Thomas Edison's invention of the light bulb in 1879, candles were the world's major source of artificial lighting.

Color Wheel

When making candles, color is key. This wheel shows how colors work with each other. The colors next to each other work together in harmony. Colors opposite each other have a stronger effect when used together because they have more contrast.

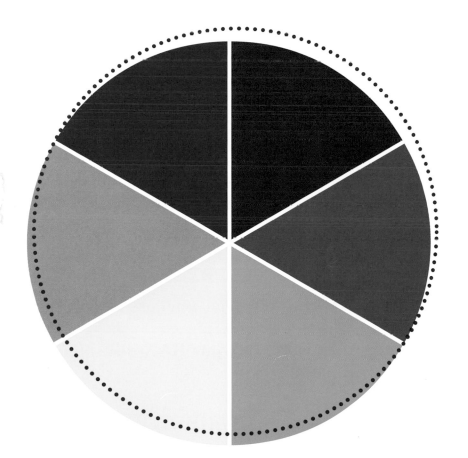

Candle Museum

The Yankee Candle Company in South Deerfield, Massachusetts, has a candle museum and Bavarian Christmas Village where visitors can learn about the history of candle making and dip their own candles.

Glossary

ball candle (BAWL KAN-duhl) ball-shaped candle with wick

beeswax (BEEZ-waks) wax sheets with honeycomb texture

cane (KANE) log-shaped, rolled strip of sheet wax

chunk wax (CHUHNGK WAKS) slabs of wax that get broken down into chunks

column candle (KOL-uhm KAN-duhl) long candle with straight sides and round ends

container candle (kuhn-TAYN-er KAN-duhl) candle with a decorative container surrounding wax

core candle (KOR KAN-duhl) center of an embedded candle

drip candle (DRIP KAN-duhl) candle that drips wax heavily

embedded candle (em-BED-ded KAN-duhl) candle with decorative materials embedded in wax

gel wax (JEL WAKS) clear, gelatin-like wax

mold (MOHLD) removable container into which hot, melted wax is poured to form a candle

pre-tabbed wick (PREE-tabd WIK) wick with a metal disk that anchors it in wax.

taper candle (TAY-pur KAN-duhl) long, thin tubular candle

wax sheet (WAKS SHEET) thin, flat wax

Read More

Eberling, Eric and Alan Wycheck. *Basic Candle Making: All the Skills and Tools You Need to Get Started.* Mechanicsburg, Pennsylvania: Stackpole Basic Books, 2002.

Scholastic Books. *Candle Making for Kids.* New York: Scholastic, 1999.

Spear, Sue. *Candle Making in a Weekend: Inspirational Ideas and Practical Projects.* Cincinnati, Ohio: North Light Books, 1999.

Internet Sites

FactHound offers a safe, fun way to find Internet sites related to this book. All of the sites on FactHound have been researched by our staff.

Here's how

1. Visit *www.facthound.com*
2. Type in this special code **0736843833** for age-appropriate sites. Or enter a search word related to this book for a more general search.
3. Click on the **Fetch It** button. FactHound will fetch the best sites for you!

About the Author

Deborah Hufford was a staff writer for *Country Home* and the former editor of *Country Handcrafts* magazine, which included a regular craft column called "Kids' Korner." She was also the crafts editor for *McMagazine,* a magazine created for McDonald's Corporation. Most recently she served as the associate publisher for two of the country's leading craft magazines, *Bead & Button* and *Dollhouse Miniatures*, as well as a book division of crafts titles.

Index